LAZY HOUSEKEEPING GUIDE

CLAIRE ALEEN

Cover design by James, GoOnWrite.com

by any means, electronic or mechanical, including photocopying, recording, or by any information storage and retrieval system, without permission in writing from the publisher.

ISBN: 978-0-9899143-8-3

ACKNOWLEDGMENTS

To Circle, my cat. Hopefully this book will make the upkeep of your litter box easier.

CONTENTS

INTRODUCTION

When I wake up in the morning, I want to go right back to sleep. I don't have any strange sleeping disorders. And the problem isn't that I'm tired. It's mostly that I'm lazy. My perfect day would go something like this:

Wake up (at 2PM)

Watch funny videos on my iPad in bed for three hours

Order a pizza and ensure that the delivery driver has access to my home so that he can deliver the pizza directly to my bed. He would also bring lots of napkins because I'm a sloppy eater and I hate food on my face.

Get up and drink tea, because I don't want to get bedsores

Go back to sleep for a nice three

hour nap

.

Wake up and play video games and browse the web until 3AM

Repeat and do it all again

Did you see house cleaning any-where in that ideal day list? Neither did I. I don't like to clean. I just want to log on to Pinterest and stuff my face with French fries and chicken nuggets. Unfortunately, my days are anything but ideal. My real day goes something like this:

Wake up at 7AM

Go to work

Go home famished and continue to work

Complain about my job

Head to the store for a lottery ticket

Try and contact a few friends via text message or phone so that I have some semblance of a social life

Go to bed at 2AM utterly exhausted and wishing I could have crawled into bed at nine.

There are two lessons to be learned here. The first lesson is don't work. And the second lesson is – I still didn't mention cleaning my home, and this book is supposed to be about a lazy girl's guide to cleaning. The reason I didn't mention cleaning is simple. I don't do much of it. And my house isn't an utter disaster zone, contrary to what you might think. Even with laziness and apathy it remains roach-free and if I were to have company over I would only need ten minutes to pick up a few things here and there. I wouldn't die of embarrassment from an impromptu visit because of the way my living area looks.

But the fact still remains that I hate to clean. Dirty dishes and sticky floors annoy me and I've found that since I work nonstop without breaks or vacation – my house is almost always on the precipice of pure chaos. It's both baffling and troubling how quickly the sink tends to fill. Sometimes I daydream about someone inventing a self-cleaning house.

There are self-cleaning ovens, but when it comes to homes, the burden still falls squarely on the shoulders of the homeowner – as if paying a hefty mortgage and ridiculous taxes aren't enough. Homeowners have to keep their homes pretty, lest their property depreciates and they find themselves underwater.

However, don't despair, a clean home is possible without investing hours scrubbing toilets and counters. You just have to figure out how to do things quickly and efficiently. If we are brilliant enough in our technological age to create keyboard shortcuts, surely we can create some shortcuts to clean our homes. And these shortcuts shouldn't leave us feeling drained and exhausted. This book will teach you how to have a cleaner home while investing less time. This book is for the lazy girls out there who really don't want to clean but feel like they have to if they want to maintain some sanity in their homes.

I created this guide for women (and men) who have enough psychological self-awareness and enough authenticity to admit that they are lazy. My admiration goes to you for not living in denial. You purchased this book because you're tired of cleaning all the time. Or you purchased this book because you never clean, but would actually like to. Or you purchased this book because you're looking for useful tips that make life easier in the house-keeping department.

And maybe you've noticed that I've

called this guide the Lazy Girl's House-keeping Guide. I decided to help the ladies because I've learned that lazy men don't need guides. They don't need guides because lazy men get a wife. They don't work on their housekeeping skills, they just find someone who will marry them and put up with their laziness. Some women manage to pull this scheme off and find men who agree to take on all the cleaning and chores, but these women are the exception. The rest of us are on our own and unless we are willing to shell out the cash for a housekeeper, most of us have to simply find the time to do the cleaning ourselves.

And I didn't just write this book for you – I wrote this book for myself. I also needed a kick in the butt as far as my home was concerned. Like most people, I very much enjoy living in a clean and beautiful space. And like most people I don't enjoy the drudgery involved in creating a clean and beautiful space. So, I wrote this book on a quest to find tips and advice that would be useful to me in creating the home and haven that my family would come to appreciate – a clean and beautiful home full of not just love, but a sink devoid of dirty dishes.

I hope that by the end of this book, your sink will also have fewer dishes. Let's get started.

1 THE PERFECT HOME

"Excuse the mess, but we live here."
- Roseanne Barr

The idea of the perfect house is lunacy. There is no such thing. If a home is perfect, spotless and beautifully clean (museum immaculate) then there are two things going on. Either it's a model home, and no one actually lives there, or the owner's name is Oprah. Unless you have decided to let your home sit vacant or you're a billionaire then there is a good chance that your home isn't perfect. Nor should it be. A perfect home doesn't exist, and this is the first step to getting on the path to a cleaner home.

We have to blame some of this on our culture. Let's face it – if you live in America then you are probably aware that most of America suffers from a bit of germaphobia. Americans have a reputation of being afraid of bacteria and we get that reputation from our constant disinfecting and sanitizing practices. And while it is true that in some cases the germaphobia is unwarranted and uptight, we also have to remember that bubonic plagues once stalked the streets in our less than sterilized times. It was those plagues that led to what some see as an over-sanitized world.

But even the typical sanitized American home isn't perfect. If you have friends who live in homes that always seem spotless and you think my assumption about model homes and billionaire living is incorrect, I'll let you in on a secret. Any friend you visit that has a spotless home was rushing around cleaning up before you got there. Or they just finished cleaning and then you showed up. And if this isn't the case and your friend just somehow manages to keep their home completely spotless, then I don't know what else to say – other than it's like the time I discovered that some people actually get dressed every day - even on days when they don't leave the house. I thought that stuff only happened on TV.

But in the real world, Pottery Barn homes only exist in the Pottery Barn catalog. And the sooner we let go of this notion that our home should be perfect, the better off we'll all be. Perfect homes are making millions of women (and men) feel inadequate. It's how many people feel when they open up a *Southern Living* or *Architectural Digest* magazine only to compare some swanky living area next to their own thrift market finds with the scratches and scuffs. It's not just the magazines that are notorious for falsely portraying the perfect home in a setting that is purely mythical. Television shows more often than not set their characters in beautifully decorated and spotlessly clean homes.

It's a farce, don't believe it.

2 THE CLOSET

The closet is your best friend. And while we are talking about the closet I should probably mention that this book isn't about having a spotless home. This book is about having a home that is presentable. A home in which you feel happy and proud to call your own. A home in which you are not embarrassed to entertain impromptu visitors. You can have this home, but you've first got to get friendly with your closet.

If your closet is overstuffed with clothes, the first thing that you'll have to do is pare down your wardrobe. You don't need eighty-five Christmas sweaters. Matter of fact, get rid of all your Christmas sweaters because Christmas sweaters are ugly – all of those reindeer noses, wreathes, and elves are just plain tacky. But I digress.

Lazy girls understand the hidden power of the closet, and they understand that the closet has deep esoteric meaning.

There is a reason for the phrases "skeletons in the closet" and "coming out of the closet." And isn't it clear why the boogie man lives in the closet? Because the closet is the perfect place to hide stuff. For those of us with too much on our plate and very little time to clean, the closet is the hiding place for our less than stellar housekeeping habits. I would tell you to sweep things under the rug, but the bulk would just make your place look crazy and cause your family and guests to trip over stuff.

Instead, use your closet. Shove everything in there.

I find that going throughout the house with a basket and picking up everything that is out of place is a great, easy way to sweep the house clean with-out having to put too much thought into where things are actually supposed to be. It gives your house an almost instanta-neous tidying without the tedious process of eyeing every stray piece of paper or object and putting it 'exactly' where it's supposed to go.

So pick up a basket and start "cleaning." Not everyone will be able to get by with one basket. Some people will need two. Once you've done your basket pickup simply place those baskets in the closet. You can always go through them another time. Or, you could never go through them, and only rummage through them when you realize that the book you were reading in your living area is no longer on the floor where you left it. So, it must be in that closet basket.

3 USE IT OR LOSE IT

"Have nothing in your home that you do not know to be useful or believe to be beautiful."
- William Morris

I've found that one of the best ways to tackle clutter and get rid of all the excess that makes my home more chaotic is to simply get rid of stuff. I love to purge. I've been the girl in the airport with two pieces of luggage that contained every single thing that she owned. I've never really been a fan of clutter. I think homes are the most beautiful when they are simplistic. I find clean lines, open, empty spaces, and a lack of furniture very appealing.

I think the best living areas are the ones where there is enough room to do a cartwheel. I like using the idea of the "cartwheel rule" to discover whether or not your living space is indeed over-crowded. If you can't do a cartwheel in your space without injuring your knees and head then it's probably too cluttered. Now, I understand not everyone is blessed in the square footage depart-ment. And those who live in Manhattan and San Francisco (or are just poor) are exceptions to the rule – but the average American has enough space to do a cartwheel in their living area and still live comfortably. Unfortunately, many Ameri-cans can't do cartwheels in their living ar-eas without injuring themselves because of furniture or other objects that are taking up entirely too much space.

If you can't do a cartwheel in your living area, then it's time to reevaluate what you have in your home and ask yourself if you really need it.

But we should also consider that it's not really the larger items that keep us cleaning all day – it's the little things that mess it all up. Your bigger furniture may not necessarily be the enemy. That antique table, bookshelf or old rocking chair may not add as much despair to your life as you think. The real problems are books, binders, pieces of mail, Kleenex boxes, pens, cups, plates, headphones, coins, water bottles, scarves, bracelets, watches, journals, notepads and paper clips. It's these things that have a tendency to drive us crazy. Get rid of it all… seriously. Wendell Berry once said, "Don't own so much clutter that you will be relieved to see your house catch fire." I agree with Mr. Berry.

The less stuff you have, the easier it is to clean. And this principle of simplicity can even work for items that we think we "need." In the past when I literally owned one coffee mug – it was impossible for my sink to fill up with dishes – I simply didn't own enough dishes. I also (at the time) was eating like a cow, so I was continually frustrated that I had to perpetually wash the few dishes I had. But my house was cleaner. And yours can be too if you simply get rid of everything that you don't really need.

It is true that the cleanest homes are the most simplistic. People without children or hobbies have the cleanest homes of all – if they keep it simple, and are not pack rats. But collecting anything, working on anything, and children in the house in general are one way to have a home that's in complete chaos. And I understand that as far as hobbies are concerned, some people have enough money to own or lease a place that allows them to have an entire room dedicated to their hobby. But the rest of the poor, middle-class world is finding that working at the dining room table is about as good as it's going to get. Here is the lesson: if you want to have a clean house, don't have children or hobbies.

I love the idea of placing things into three categories – beautiful, useful and trash. Go through your home and get rid of anything that isn't beautiful or useful. You can keep the pretty painting and the coffee-table sized Webster's dictionary while throwing out old *Vanity Fair* maga-zines and the hideous clock your co-worker bought you last Christmas. If you will decide not to have anything in your house that you do not feel to be beautiful or useful, your purging process will go a lot smoother. You won't have to deliberate about whether or not you should keep something. And if you are unsure about something – trash it. The things that are the most meaningful are things that you won't have to think twice about.

Purging is a great way to get a

house in better shape and cut down on your chores. The rule is simple: the less stuff that you have in your house, the less housework you'll have to do. So get rid of clutter and junk.

But before you pitch everything in the trash, first consider whether your stuff is worth giving to charity. Places like the Salvation Army and other nonprofits who help the less fortunate are always looking for clothes, furniture, and other items that could be truly useful to someone else. Furthermore, most of these places will also give you a tax deduction for your contribution. Everyone wins. If you aren't feeling too lazy, you may even consider having a yard sale. Get your junk together and get rid of it by selling it to someone who thinks your trash is treasure.

And get rid of any improper notions that you must hang on to your things be-cause they somehow make you happy.

Researchers have proven time and time again that things don't make us happy. They have discovered that healthy relationships and great experiences make us happy.

4 WHY MAKE YOUR BED?

Now, I understand that there is something about a made up bed that makes a room feel so much more pulled together. People understand that in the bedroom, the bed is the central component. It's like the anchor of the room by which everything else is grounded. So it makes sense that if you want a beautiful and pulled together bedroom, then you'll need to make the bed. And I agree to a certain extent.

But it really does seem counterintuitive to make a bed that you plan to hop right back into. I mean, after all, you do have to get back in your bed at the end of the day.

And if you are as lazy as me, then you don't even want to pull the sheets back when you climb in the bed. You might even stand there for a moment and stare at those sheets somehow hoping that they will pull themselves back for you so that you can just hop in the bed and go to sleep.

Sheets don't pull themselves back. And because we have already established the bed as the anchor of the room – then it is somewhat important that the bed looks nice. But we have also agreed that making a bed is absolutely counterintuitive and doesn't really help you since you are just going to mess it up again later.

The solution is a very, very large duvet cover that you can throw over the sheets and pillows. You don't even have to touch the sheets or rearrange the pillows so that they are perfectly against the headboard (or wall). Just toss that duvet over the bed and hope for the best. You've covered your shame. That's all you need for now.

Nearly 59% of people don't make their bed. Around 27% actually make their bed and the other 12% pay a housekeeper to make it for them. I very much wish I could be that 12 percent.

And while it may seem like a relief that most people aren't making their beds, the bad news is that there are serious lifestyle and happiness differences between people who make their beds and those who don't. Bed makers are more likely to own their homes, like their jobs and exercise regularly. Non-bed makers spend most of their time at protest marches, hate their jobs and often complain about the cost of a latte.

Scientific research has also confirmed that spending a few minutes making your bed in the morning can make you more productive. So if you are of the mindset that no one will see your bed ex-

cept for your immediate family, and making your bed is a waste of time, at least
cover those crumpled sheets and spread
the duvet cover over the mess –

for productivity's sake.

5 HOUSEHOLD TOOLS THAT SAVE THE DAY

Below is a list of household tools that you'll need:

A vacuum. The vacuum is your friend, and if you are very lazy you need your vacuum to come in two sizes – small and large. And if you are extra lazy, you'll use that small one a lot more than you use the large one. The small one, also lovingly referred to as the DustBuster is the go-to vacuum for people who don't feel like lugging a heavy vacuum from a storage room or closet and burning 200 calories as they push it across the floor. Serious vacuuming (and cleaning in general) is akin to a workout. If you're doing it right, you may work up a sweat. Which is why most of us hate cleaning, because cleaning is truly work – and not the white-collar kind. It's the back-breaking blue-collar kind. Use your handheld vacuum for picking up the small spots of dirt obvious to the eye. This will give you the appearance of a cleaner home while being less laborious than using a larger vacuum. Small vacuums are also great for tackling counter and coffee table crumbs.

A large wash cloth. Use it for wiping any and everything. If something is particularly stubborn a cloth soaked in hot water is the most amazing cleaning tool on earth. Some people prefer a microfiber cleaning cloth. They are relatively inexpensive and come in packs.

A steam mop. If you don't have one, get one. If you live in a primarily carpeted space, reread the paragraph on dust-busting. I actually enjoy cleaning my floors on my hands and knees. It's archaic and the antithesis of everything I believe in as far as cleaning is concerned. And although I still prefer to clean on my hands and knees, I have to admit that the first time I used a steam mop I heard the Hallelujah chorus. It really does make life and cleaning much easier when steam and towels are combined in a way that makes it easier for you to sweep across your floors. And because steam mops are lighter than vacuums they are less labor intensive. You don't burn as many calories when you're gliding a mop across the floor. You probably only burn about 50 – these estimates may vary based on home and belly sizes. If you don't have a steam mop in your home, then you might as well get rid of your cell phone. Because steam mops are just as innovative and necessary as cell phones. People wonder all the time as they stand in Apple store lines "What in the world did we do before cell phones?" Once you get a steam mop you too will ask yourself "What in the world did I do before the steam mop?" I can tell you exactly what you did before the steam mop. You did one of three things. You may not have done anything at all, and allowed your floors to get stickier and grosser by the hour. Or perhaps your floors weren't sticky, but I assure you they were still gross. Or you used a mop. I must say this; mop water is the nastiest water on the face of the planet. You basically swing a mop across your floors spreading more dirt and debris. Your floors become a Petri dish when you use a mop. Or you got down on your hands and knees (like I do) and enraged every feminist in a 50-mile radius as you scrubbed those floors with all your might. You don't have to do any of those things anymore if you can just simply shell out the bucks to get a steam mop.

A supply caddy. Buy a container with a handle (or without one) that allows you to easily dump everything into it and use that to shuffle your supplies back and forth with ease. Keep your disinfectant sprays, sponges, microfiber cloths, squeegees and whatever else suits your fancy for cleaning in your caddy. You'll shave time off the cleaning process. Anything that professional housekeepers use to keep themselves organized should also be a part of your repertoire. There are a few other things that are essential for deep cleaning and should also be in your supply caddy – alcohol which can be used as a disinfectant and makes faucets surprisingly shiny and room spray to deodorize the place. Items such as hydrogen peroxide and alcohol feel less "chemical" and are excellent for cleaning everything from door handles to carpet stains.

A supply apron. In addition to a supply caddy, you might also want to consider buying a supply apron. This isn't the girly, cute apron that you can pick up at Williams & Sonoma for twenty-five dollars. This is the thing that you have to hunt for and will likely purchase on Amazon. The difference between the supply apron and a kitchen apron is practicality. A supply apron has several extremely deep pockets meant for carrying around tools and household cleaning supplies.

Disinfectant. Some people like to use wipes, and find that they make a home feel and smell really clean. In the past, I used a popular brand of disinfectant wipes until I realized that they were laden with chemicals that were making me sick. Fortunately, you can buy all natural disinfectant wipes that aren't full of harsh chemicals. If you are willing to invest just a little extra time - consider making your own disinfectant wipes. To make your own you'll need an old baby wipe box, tea tree oil, distilled vinegar and cloth rags. You can use old shredded t-shirts for cloths. If you want some scent you can even add an essential oil. Soak the wipes in a mixture of two cups of white vinegar and a few drops of tea tree and essential oils. Squeeze out the excess liquid and fold the wipes into your container.

Paper towels. I use lots of these in my home, which means I am not as eco-friendly as I'd like to be. But, hey I'm working on it. Baby steps, OK? I use paper towels to clean everything from floors to counters.

Toilet scrubbers with disposable cleaning heads. Let's admit it, the other toilet brushes are disgusting. Unless you are pouring alcohol (91%) over the toilet brush after you use it, it's just sitting there with fecal matter all over it. I prefer my fecal matter in the trash or down the toilet drain – not sitting next to my shower. Where do you prefer to keep your fecal matter?

6 UNBREAKABLE RULES

An unbreakable rule is something that you do each day no matter what. It's something that you commit yourself to no matter what. For instance, one of my unbreakable rules is to brush my teeth and shower each day. No matter how lazy or icky I'm feeling I manage to accomplish these two tasks. Consider the things that you do every single day no matter what. Things that you are programmed to do. Maybe it's hygienic like taking a bath or maybe it's a health thing like taking a vitamin. Now it's time to add a new unbreakable rule in the area of housekeeping.

Some people already have unbreakable rules in regards to housekeeping. The most famous one is a made bed. Some people just have to make their bed in the morning, even if they never get to the dishes or laundry. Others have the habit of straightening their workspace each day while others might ensure that they always wipe down their kitchen counters in the evening.

It doesn't matter what your un-breakable housekeeping rule is – what matters is that you have one. Find some-thing that you want to accomplish every day and simply start doing it. And keep it simple. Simplicity will give you a better chance of falling into a routine that is diffi-cult to fall out of.

7 7-MINUTE HOUSEKEEPING

*"I choose a lazy person to do a hard job.
Because a lazy person will find an easy
way to do it."*
- Bill Gates

For many lazy girls, one of the off-shoots of laziness lies in procrastination. Lazy people are notoriously horrible procrastinators – waiting till the very last minute to do things and then throwing something together once the timer has ticked away and hoping that it works. For this reason, lazy girls don't clean until they really have to. And if they are especially lazy, all cleaning sessions may hinge on guests coming over.

The impromptu guest is the lazy housekeepers worst enemy. Guests who normally know how to keep their house clean usually don't have any qualms about stopping by someone's house without notice, because they assume (in their ignorance) that everyone is just like them. Of course, lazy girls know that their home is often in C.H.A.O.S – can't have anyone over soon.

However, one of the cures for laziness and procrastination is the beloved timer. There is something about a timer that poses a challenge that many competitive-minded people can't resist, and using the timer can actually be fun if done correctly. And we could all use a bit more fun.

The rule is simple. Set a timer for seven minutes (it could be more or less depending on your mood) and allot that time to cleaning. You may not get as much done as you like, but it's a start, and sometimes the cure to laziness and procrastination is to simply get going. The law of inertia states that a thing at rest stays at rest, which is why movement is so important. It's the antithesis of laziness.

I once read about a woman who had made a considerable amount of money writing books, but also managed to be the ideal wife and mother – always keeping her home spotless and her children happy. How did she do it all? She claims that she never, ever rested. She made it a point to stay on her feet all day long. I'm assuming that she did her writing at night when things were a little bit more settled and the house was quiet. She says that when her husband would call her from work and ask how her day was going, her usual reply was "I haven't sat down all day."

I once worked at a job where I had to stand on my feet all day and I will tell you this – it was utterly exhausting.

Standing on your feet is tiring. It requires a considerable amount of energy and is also a mental drain. Those who stand on their feet all day often pine for one thing – to eventually get off of them. To be able to go home and sit down, put their feet up, and sip a peppermint latte or tea. Being on your feet may be exhausting, but it can also combat laziness and maybe even procrastination. You are an object that is not at rest when you're on your feet and moving.

Setting a timer works because of several reasons. First, there is the psychological aspect. You're acknowledging that time is happening – real time – and time is the greatest commodity of all – so we become more conscientious and aware of what we are doing when we are actually measuring this commodity. Which is why every lazy girl should own a watch… or two. Of course, many lazy girls don't like watches. But I've discov-

ered this – a lot of really successful people have watch-laden wrists. They are
aware of time.

If you want to be playful you can
buy an hourglass or one of those cute
kitchen timers shaped like a piece of fruit.
Of course, you could also just use your
iPhone or even the microwave to achieve
what you need to accomplish. The point is
to set a timer for at least seven minutes
and start cleaning.

8 PAPER PLATES AND CUPS

And this mess is so big and so deep and so tall, we cannot pick it up. There is no way at all!
- Dr. Seuss, The Cat in the Hat

The environment will have to take one for the team. Climate change and saving trees aside, paper plates and cups may be a great option for you – especially if you have a deep trash can. If you don't have a deep trash can I suggest getting one because there is nothing nastier than trash that is filled to the brim.

Using paper plates and paper cups are going to significantly reduce the amount of dishes that you use. Just don't buy those plastic beer cups that you see in fraternity houses. You don't want your house resembling a frat house. Of course, paper plates and cups have a couple of drawbacks. First, they don't work for everything. It's hard to have a hot cup of coffee in a paper cup – unless you want to burn your finger tips. Second, paper plates and cups may reduce the amount of dishes in your sink, but they add to your trash pile, creating a big heaping mess. This isn't good at all – especially if you don't take your trash out often and you're busy growing penicillin in there. Finally, paper plates and cups could get expensive. But, I want you to consider whether or not it's cheaper than a maid… and therapy.

9 LEARN FROM PROFESSIONALS

You can cut the time that you spend cleaning your house if you start to examine what the professionals are doing and take notes. Professional housekeepers (especially those who work in hotels) have to clean thoroughly and quickly – probably with more emphasis on the quick than thorough. For that reason, they are prime for observation when it comes to cleaning. The top professionals – those who have been in the hospitality industry for a while know how to clean quickly without sacrificing quality. So, what are they doing? Here are a few things professionals do:

Don't focus on one area – clean everything. Cleaning one room at a time is called zone cleaning, and it's a great way to keep your overall home filthy if you are a lazy girl. Zone cleaning isn't really productive, and it's not wise to focus on one tiny area and forget about the elephants hanging out in the other room. You need to tackle more than just baby elephants – mama and papa elephant need to be shuffled out of your other living spaces.

In a *Woman's Day* article, Lisa Romero, owner of Just Like New Cleaning in Fort Collins, Colorado said "You can either clean your kitchen in four hours, or clean your entire house top to bottom in four hours," and I have to agree. Instead of focusing so much energy in one space, spread your energy out. If you do this, this will help you work quicker and more efficiently, and it will also give the overall cleaning process a bit more continuity. Also, I don't recommend cleaning your home for four straight hours.

Part of the reason you're probably

reading the *Lazy Girl's Housekeeping Guide* is because you feel stuck. And if you feel stuck, then you probably have done your fair share of zone cleaning, because that is what many stuck people do – focus too much energy on one particular area while the rest of the mud around them is turning to quicksand. Of course, if you focus all of your effort cleaning your office desk, you may not ever dust the bookshelves, or any other part of the house.

However, a sister of zone cleaning, which is called "task cleaning" can actually be helpful. Zone cleaning, as we defined earlier is spending an inordinate amount of time on one space or room. Task cleaning, on the other hand is spending time throughout the entire home on one task. So, for example, you may decide to vacuum every room in your house instead of just the bedroom. Many experts are in favor of task cleaning while

the general consensus is that zone cleaning is a no-no.

So instead of supplying too much
energy to one space of your home –
make sure that you are spreading the
love.

**Another thing that professional
housekeepers do is clean top to bottom**. You're supposed to start at the top
rim, as close as possible to anything near
the ceiling. But instead of stepping on a
ladder to clear the dust bunnies at the top
– we are going to avoid that stuff altogether. There is no need to bring attention
to areas that you can't really see anyway.
You want to focus on what can be seen.

Clean left to right. This keeps you
from skipping over anything in the room
that may have otherwise been neglected.

Clean what your eyes can see.
Don't worry about all the little corners and

crevices of your home. They will some-how take care of themselves, and you'll know that they are ready for a good cleaning when you see spider webs in the corner. Let spider webs be your cue to take the time to clean those areas. Just focus on cleaning what your eyes can see. Scan the floors and shelves and counters for things that draw the eye. Maybe it's a wine glass on the coffee ta-ble that is making the entire space look disheveled, or maybe it's a knick-knack that somehow fell on the floor and has become an obstacle. Don't worry about anything else other than what draws the eye.

Let cleansers do the work for you. If you get the right cleanser you'll find that you'll have less on your plate. A good cleansing product will require a spray and sit. As the cleanser sits you can sit too. Many professional house-keepers will spray cleansing solution on surfaces in a room and walk right out of the room to go work on something else. They'll come back half an hour later and just wipe. They've allowed the cleanser to do all the work for them so that their part of the process is easier.

Reward yourself. The reason that professional housekeepers do such a great job at cleaning a home or a hotel room (besides the fact that many have training and years of experience) is that there is a financial incentive involved. They are going to collect a paycheck that will reward them for their work. This gives them the strength to get that toilet brush out, when they really don't feel like it.

Sometimes you simply have to reward yourself. Trick your brain a little bit. Maybe you need to tell yourself that you'll get a Krispy Kreme donut in the morning if you vacuum the hallway. Or use your favorite TV show as an incentive – don't allow yourself to watch it until you've done what you need to do in your home.

Rewarding yourself requires some open and well-thought out reverse psychology, but I'm confident you can get your brain to do what you want to do so that it can get what it wants.

10 TV TIME

One thing that I've found really helpful is to use commercial breaks productively. On average, Americans watch at least a couple of hours of television a day – and a significant portion of that television watching involves sitting through commercials. You don't need to know about Walmart's latest deal or the Ford Pickup Year End sale. Instead, get up during those commercial breaks and clean.

On average, commercial breaks last a few minutes. A few minutes may not seem like a lot of time. But believe me – it's plenty. Especially if you haven't previously been spending a few minutes each day cleaning your house. Those commercial break minutes add up, and before you know it – you've invested a half hour cleaning your house, and it's already starting to look better.

Use commercial breaks to get things done. If you start using the commercial break rule – you may find that you are getting a lot of stuff done during the Fall season when all of the new premieres of your favorite shows start. If you are tempted to TIVO or use some other device to skip over the commercials entirely don't do it – you are forfeiting valuable time that you could have spent cleaning.

If you like the show enough – you'll make sure that you schedule the time to watch it. And by scheduling the time to watch that show – you are simultaneously scheduling time to clean. I've seen other writers advise readers to use commercial breaks to work out (squeezing in some sit-ups) and I even saw one writer advise his readers on what games to play during commercial breaks. You don't have time to workout and play games. You've got a dirty house to clean. So use those commercial breaks to get it done.

Using a commercial break is called micro-productivity, because you are using a small portion of time to accomplish a bigger goal. For some, the secret to a really clean house is to watch more TV and employ micro-productivity.

11 CLEANING CLOTHES

Some people will actually go to the gym if they simply put on their workout clothes. Maybe this can work for you too. The idea is to essentially wear a cleaning outfit. Maybe a pair of overalls (do you actually own a pair?) or something ruggedly awful and comfortable. Just find something you can comfortably clean in and then designate that as your uniform.

Professional housekeepers often wear a uniform. It reminds them that they have a job to do, but they also know it's easier to clean with knee pads. Find something easily washable, and then use that as your cleaning uniform. This tip may not work for everyone because the clothes should be comfortable, and for some, comfortable clothing could just bring out more laziness.

However, if you like the idea of setting up a uniform for your cleaning routine, but don't know if you would actually get your cleaning done despite wearing a uniform, add an essential item to the uniform to solidify things – an apron. The apron can be as simplistic, utilitarian or as beautiful as you want. I suggest using a supply apron. Put your cleaning clothes on, and then wrap the apron around you as your final piece and feel a little bit more motivated to clean.

12 DIRTY LAUNDRY

I like the color pink. But I haven't always liked pink. Especially not the weird pink color that invades all of your white clothes when you decide to haphazardly wash your clothes together. That pink is usually a freakish and bizarre shade.

Fortunately, there is a way that you can avoid the weird pink or blue clothes that actually shouldn't be pink or blue because they are supposed to be white. You can wash all of your clothes together with your machine set on cold. And if you want to save even more time stop using detergent and dryer sheets. I barely use either – both are rubbish and a way to extort money and line the pockets of the laundry illuminati. It's not really necessary to use detergent and most people use too much detergent on their clothes, without even realizing it.

Believe it or not your clothes can come out pretty clean just by washing them in water. And static dryer sheets aren't really necessary unless you have a bunch of silky or satin clothes and it's winter.

If you have a piece of brand new clothing, then that's another story. You're probably worried about bleeding so you may want to be careful about how you wash that particular garment. At least until the newness has worn off and you become as apathetic towards it as the rest of your clothes.

13 BAKE OR GET SMART

If you don't want to worry about the cleanliness of your home, learn how to bake or get smart quickly. This tip may seem a little out of place in a guide about cleaning your house in a lazy kind of way, but it's here for good reason. And the reason is this: it's really hard for people to care about how disheveled your home is when it smells like fresh baked cookies.

The smell of fresh brownies, cookies or cinnamon rolls gives you a legitimate excuse not to clean. How can you clean when you're busy baking yummy stuff. Nobody really likes to hang around a dirty house, but if that dirty house smells like chocolate (that will be in their stomach shortly), I'm sure they'll be willing to look past the chaos.

If you don't know how to bake,

learn. Cookies are the easiest thing to make, and you can just pick them up in the produce section of the store. Pre-made cookie dough requires little effort. Just take it out of the package, place it in small round balls and put it on a baking sheet for fifteen to twenty minutes.

Next time you have company coming over get the oven preheated for your cookies. And if you are by yourself with no company coming and simply exhausted by the clutter of your home, bake some cookies for yourself. You'll feel better.

It isn't just freshly baked goods that earn the favor of company and keep them from judging the cleanliness of your home. People also tend to overlook a lot of stuff when genius is involved. Albert Einstein is a stunning example of how people are willing to overlook appearance for the sake of brilliance. Einstein's genius compensated for his unkempt appearance, and you can compensate for your less than clean house with your book smarts.

Get a dictionary and learn some new words – words that no one will understand except for you. Words that are so eloquent and intelligent it makes you sound as if you are speaking in a foreign language when you use them. And find a way to wiggle those words into your conversations. Also, read as much academic material as you can get your hands on. Yes, it might feel a little tiring to go over textbooks, and it's very likely that you wanted to leave college completely in the past – but just make this small investment now – spending a couple of weeks reading, so that you can allow your inner genius to emerge and not have to clean your house for the rest of the year.

And if someone comes over, immediately impress and confuse them with your new vocabulary. They'll stand or sit there spending so much time trying to figure out what you're saying and wondering how you became so bright that they'll forget they are actually sitting next to a pair of soiled underwear.

I don't know what it is about geniuses, but people are willing to excuse their bad behavior, their unkempt appearance and their messy homes simply because they are so incredibly smart. It's kind of like being super-duper beautiful. People are willing to overlook other personal faults if a person is gorgeous enough. And while I do suggest reading and learning new things specifically to impress people, I do not recommend transforming into a Barbie doll so that people don't care about what your apartment looks like. Skimming a few textbooks and learning some new words is a one-time thing. But beauty takes continual effort. Unless you naturally have it, you'll have to fight with a blow dryer, uncomfortable clothes and makeup every day, which is just too tedious and complicated for a lazy girl.

14 ROUTINE

This isn't going to work for every-one. Some people love routines while others loathe them. If you are in the second category, you may want to skip over this chapter altogether as it's just going to cause you to become more resentful by the day as you establish a routine in your life that you hate.

But even the most free-spirited and wild of us like some semblance of structure. And even when our lives feel chaotic and spontaneous if we dig deeply enough and examine our days I'm sure that we can find something that we do almost every day religiously. It could be as simple as checking our email every single morning or eating a piece of chocolate in the evening.

So establishing a little structure in

your cleaning routine may not be as diffi-cult as you think. Of course, cleaning is not as enjoyable as eating chocolate or checking email, but it can become such an integral part of your routine that you no longer notice it infringing on your day. The best way to establish a cleaning routine is to start small. If you say that you are go-ing to vacuum the entire house every day in the evening, you are overreaching. But if you decide to put a few dishes in the dishwasher every evening – you're get-ting somewhere. You're making progress.

15 SHOES AND TOILETS

The toilet is by far the most disgusting thing in any house, and for many it's the most dreaded thing to clean. The housekeeping and hospitality industry have made millions primarily because of the porcelain throne. Even people who say that they enjoy cleaning (and are clearly lying) do not want to clean a toilet.

If you are a hippy that believes that if it's yellow then you should let it mellow, then you understand the full capacity of the toilet's wrath. If left unattended, toilets will grow colonies of bacteria, mold, fungus, and every conceivable germ imaginable. If you don't care for it properly, it will begin to cultivate its very own ecosystem.

If you and your family have excellent transit times – 'transit time' is the time it takes to have a pee or poop after eating

– then you probably need more help than your constipated counterparts when it comes to keeping the toilet clean. It should also be noted that most Americans are chronically constipated and don't even know it. One trick to cleaning your toilet is to use a slice of Magic Eraser. Drop a slice of that into the toilet and let it sit there overnight to do the dirty work for you. You should discover that you are spending less time cleaning your toilet.

Another way to keep your toilet clean is to tell your man to pee while sitting down. If you don't have a man (and you are a woman), then you should also pee while sitting down. Not only will your toilet become slightly less gross, but your entire bathroom will benefit from the reduction of pee particles splashing up and away from the toilet and landing in and around everything that is near the toilet.

The Swedes have managed to get

the toilet problem right. A political party in Sweden tabled a motion to ban urinals in the country's office bathrooms. The reason the Swedes thought it would benefit men to sit was because of prostrate health. When men sit down, they empty their bladders more efficiently, and there is less excess waste hovering around in their insides. Apparently, men who sit down on the toilet also have longer and healthier sex lives. The Swedes say so.

But the Swedish would also get another added benefit by seating their men. They would have cleaner toilets. So ask your man to sit down and pee and if he tells you that his masculinity requires him to stand up, just tell him that his prostrate will fall out of his body if he doesn't start sitting on the toilet.

While we are on the topic of Europeans, let's discuss shoe removal. In many European countries (and Canada too), people take off their shoes. It's common courtesy (and common sense) for Europeans to leave their shoes at the door. They don't like the idea of tracking mud, dirt, debris, or germs through someone's home, so they take off their shoes upon entrance. While Americans believe in wearing shoes inside the house, it would actually be more American (and by American I mean germophobic) to take your shoes off.

Not only will your house be cleaner, but you'll also reduce the amount of bacterium creeping into the bedroom on the soles of your shoes. You create not just a cleaner environment, but a healthier one by removing your shoes.

16 MAKE CLEANING EASIER

"Housework, if done right, can kill you."
- Erma Bombeck

Sometimes you just need a few "aha" moments to help you realize the folly of your housecleaning ways. We all have those times where we run into something amazing and think "Why didn't I think of that?" Well here are a few things that you may not have thought of that is going to make housekeeping a little bit easier and a little bit lazier for you:

Use plastic wrap on the shelves of your refrigerator. The fridge is one of the most dreaded things to clean. It's bad enough that you have to sponge away old food, but you also have to do it while your fingers are cold. The solution: plastic wrap. Place a layer of plastic wrap on your shelves and when they become icky, just change the liner out. Your fridge will feel good as new without excessive cleaning. Now, it's just a matter of taking stuff out of the fridge and merely putting it back. And while you're in the fridge, use baking soda to absorb any odors in your fridge.

Put water in your microwave. Turn it on and let the steam do the work. If you get that microwave nice and steamy you won't have to put so much elbow grease into your scrubbing. You'll be able to simply give it a quick wipe or two while the steam has already done the job for you.

There is a such thing as a removable oven liner. Until recently, I didn't know such a glorious thing existed. But sure enough, it's not the stuff of leprechauns and fairy tales. It actually does exist, and it can make cleaning the oven a lot easier. My smoke alarm has gone off multiple times while cooking something in the oven because of food (typically cheese) sitting at the bottom. If you use a liner, you don't have to worry about burnt cheese smoking up your apartment.

Use your dishwasher to the max. The dishwasher isn't just good for cleaning dishes. It's the perfect appliance for cleaning all kinds of stuff – from rubber shoes to toys. I've even heard of someone putting their computer keyboard in the dishwasher. Of course, I wouldn't really advise you try that at home, but the other things mentioned above are fair game.

Invest in a Roomba Robot. The Roomba has been sitting in my Amazon Wishlist for as long as I can remember. There will come a day when my darling husband wants to buy me something super fancy in a blue little box. And I will reject the box and instead ask for the Roomba. A Roomba is essentially a vacuum that you don't have to push around with a handle. It cleans your floors for you – without you doing anything other than sitting on the couch and wondering why it took you so long to buy a Roomba.

Use dish mats as kitchen cabinet liners. Dishes need to dry – no problem. You can still put them away in the cabinet if you simply use dish mats as cabinet liners. Now, it could get moldy in your kitchen if you don't do this right. So the key is to leave the cabinet doors open so that there is some air circulating through the cabinet. Of course, this may not work for you if you spend a lot of time in the kitchen. Matter of fact, it could be hazardous because you might find yourself constantly bumping your head.

Clean up spills immediately. If you are really lazy your spills probably sit their awhile. You may have more than a few coffee rings on your coffee table and tea stains on the inside of your favorite mug. Cleaning up spills immediately does two things. First, it clears your mind psychologically. Knowing that you cleaned up a mess makes you feel better, and it also doesn't give the spill a chance to set in and really do damage.

Stop wasting food. If you eat what you have and don't throw it away, you'll reduce how often you have to take out the garbage, and you might also reduce the weight of your garbage bags. I'm a big proponent of minimizing waste. People waste too much – especially food and water.

Don't overuse products. You don't need a million different things to keep your home clean. A few cleaning products and tools should work just fine. Keep it simple, because the less stuff that you use to clean your house, the easier things will be and the quicker you'll be able to accomplish the job.

Get rid of odors in plastic containers. To get rid of the odor in plastic storage containers simply dissolve four tablespoons of baking soda in one quart of warm water. If the smell is still there, stuff the container with crumpled newspaper, then put a lid on it. The paper will absorb the smell. To get rid of stains in the container, mix a solution of chlorine bleach with a cup of warm water and soak it for 30 minutes.

Clean the dirtiest room first. The wisdom in tackling the dirtiest room first is that you'll still have the energy and the morale to tackle the rooms that are less dirty. As you clean, you may find that your morale steadily decreases. If you start with the toughest room, you'll be able to retain more energy to finish the rest of the

house. Finish the big stuff first, and everything else will seem easier in comparison.

17 VISUALIZE

I've read somewhere that professional athletes often use visualization techniques to win races and competitions. They see themselves accomplishing whatever it is that they have set out to do. You can do the same, along with millions of people who have harnessed the power of visualization.

Think about what you want your home to look like. Think about how beautiful and serene it will be when it's that way. This will help you start seeing some of the value in housekeeping. It's hard to complete a journey when you can't really see the destination. It's a lot like stepping out in faith – and that is precisely what visualization does – builds up our faith that we can have a clean home if we really want one.

You should start room by room. Think about what a room should look like and then allow the reality of what it actually looks like to sink in. Think about what needs to be done to that room in order for it to look that way. After you've finished visualizing - then start the cleaning process.

Visualization helps you get unstuck, and also keeps you from concentrating on one spot while the rest of the place goes to shambles.

18 MICROWAVE TIME

We all know that lazy girls have microwaves. How else would we eat? However, cooking larger meals in the microwave takes time. Sometimes it takes a full five minutes if you're cooking frozen lasagna. Fortunately, while the food is microwaving this is the perfect time to get some kitchen chores done. There are several things that you can do while your microwave runs for a couple of minutes.

Wash a couple of dishes. You may not be able to clean out your whole sink or load the dishwasher completely, but at little is better than nothing. You're making progress.

Wipe down a counter or two. It really only takes thirty seconds to wipe down a counter. It takes a full two minutes if there are dishes on your counter. After the wipe-down, your kitchen may not be completely clean, but again, you're making progress.

Clean the stove. This is especially great if your microwave is located above your stove. You can check your food and make sure the plastic bowl isn't melting while simultaneously having a less disgusting stove. This is called killing two birds with one stone.

Take your trash out. Your food might be done by the time you get back. But, again you've used your time wisely and your kitchen feels a little better because you've harnessed the power of a microwave break.

19 HOUSEPLANTS

Plants look good, they sometimes smell good, and they clean your air. You need cleaner air. Some people aren't really lazy, they are just tired, and if you're just tired, you really should invest in some houseplants. Most homes usually have poor indoor air quality. In homes where windows to the outside world are rarely opened, air quality is usually tragic. Poor air quality inside of your house causes fatigue and health concerns as well – everything from asthma to allergic reactions. But plants have a magical and marvelous way of dispelling all the nasty air that could be making you literally sick and tired.

If you aren't tired, and you're just lazy, houseplants can still work for you. Your laziness is probably turning your home into a dust bowl, and you could really use some cleaner air. So get some plants. If you don't have a 'green thumb' and you kill every plant that you come across, then I have the perfect solution – it's called bamboo. It's a beautiful plant and difficult to kill. Bamboo stalks are also fairly inexpensive and they grow like crazy. Some people actually believe that bamboo plants are lucky.

Surprisingly enough, bamboo is recommended as one of the top plants for cleaning the air. Not only that, they look good in a room and make your home a little bit more beautiful. Invest in house-plants.

20 USE COMPANY

You know that person that you would never invite over unless your house was clean. Well, this is the person you need to start inviting over more often. I've found that having company (company that you admire and maybe even want to impress) is a good place to start. It forces you to clean, and you do so, not because you really HAVE to, but because you actually WANT to.

You don't want your company to see a dirty home. You don't want them to possibly lose respect for you or contact one of those house cleaning or hoarding television shows about your situation. And for this reason, you will clean and you will be happy to do it.

The key is to invite them over once a week, preferably on the same day of each week so that you can actually try and establish a routine. You want to get into the habit of cleaning your home. And one key to make the cleaning process something you just naturally do is to form a habit.

Also, you don't necessarily have to invite one person over. Maybe you could have small parties at your place. Think about having a dinner party or movie night – both are pretty fun and both will put you in a cleaning mood.

There is one slight possible hiccup in this plan. As you invite someone over each week, there are chances that they'll decline your invitation, but the solution is to just invite someone else over. Line up about two or three people who you want to impress and start making their acquaintance. Your house will start to look nicer, and you'll also develop closer and deeper relationships in the process.

21 GROSS PLACES

It's helpful to have a clear idea of which areas in your home need the most attention. Some places are simply grimier and will make your home look and feel cleaner if you tackle the nastiest places first. Below are a few places in your home where you should dedicate more of your time.

The kitchen sink…

Kitchen sinks are disgusting. And even though the sink constantly comes in contact with hot water and soap, it's still a community of constantly partying bacteria. It's possible that your kitchen sink even has more bacteria than what you'd find on the toilets of public bathrooms – many of which are regularly cleaned with potent disinfectants. Because the sink in the kitchen has constant contact with food, most kitchen sinks are 100,000 times more contaminated than bathroom sinks. It's really important to try and keep it clean by scrubbing it down at least once a week with hot water and soap.

Your coffee maker…

Your coffee maker is also gross. I once worked in an office where the coffee maker was never cleaned. It was a boys' office with only three girls in the entire firm. Us girls banded together and decided we no longer wanted to drink gross coffee and set aside time to clean the coffee maker. It took us three days and a considerable amount of bleach, but we managed to clean it. You're supposed to wash the coffee maker every 40 to 80 brews. Washing your coffee maker should also make the coffee taste better. And who doesn't love rich, flavorful coffee? Now, I've heard the nonsense that some people believe when it comes to moldy coffee. There is actually a cult of people who refuse to clean their coffee mugs because they believe a stained mug enhances the flavor of their coffee, and also very possibly makes them grow a few extra hairs on their chest. Unfortunately, the only thing a stained coffee mug helps a person do is have frequent diarrhea. Bacteria and mold tend to accumulate in any place that hasn't been cleaned in a while, especially a place that is frequently wet. To clean your coffee maker use about four cups of vinegar. Pour the vinegar into the reservoir and let it sit for half an hour. Next, run a cycle with the vinegar and follow it up with a few more cycles until you can no longer smell the vinegar.

Your carpet…

In the book, *The Secret Life of Germs*, author Philip Tierno, Jr., PhD, explains just how disgusting carpet actually is. Unless you have the mother of all vacuum cleaners (few of us do), the average vacuums' suction doesn't reach the very bottom of the carpet, where all the bacteria actually is. There are about 200,000 soldiers of bacteria per square inch of carpet, and you are constantly feeding them. These bacteria feast on human skin cells that manage to fall on the carpet. They also eat tiny pieces of food and have been known to snack on pollen and pet dander as well. The best way to keep your carpet clean is to have a steam extraction every 18 months by a professional. If you think about it, carpet upkeep is actually quite expensive. It makes sense that you should learn to love hardwoods and tiles and start keeping that in your home, with the occasional rug from Ikea thrown in here or there.

The control dials on your stove...

Unlike the stove's surface, which is probably cleaned regularly, people forget that they need to clean the control dials. I use a disinfectant on mine. Make sure that it's nonflammable if you use a disinfectant. Clean those dials and while you're at it don't forget about all of the handles in your home, from door handles to the kitchen drawer handles to light switches and all of the other places that are routinely neglected and brimming with oily nastiness. And before you just remove the dials completely and boil them in a pot of hot water on the stove, check your stove's manual for cleaning directions.

Your toothbrush holder…

As if teeth don't already have an inherent grossness to them, your holder is crawling with more than two million cells of bacteria. I no longer use a toothbrush holder for this reason alone. Bamboo and wood are the worst offenders, and are unfortunately popular because they look good. The best material to go with when choosing a holder is either plastic or stainless steel. Both are dishwasher safe material that you can throw into the dishwasher at least once a week. And while we are at it, it's not really a good idea to have your toothbrush out in your bathroom anyway. Every time you flush your toilet (put the lid down, people) you spread germs and particles from the toilet into the air, and lots of those germs land on your beloved toothbrush. Every germaphobe worldwide recommends putting your toothbrush in a place where it's not exposed to toilet particles. Put your toothbrush in the medicine cabinet, if you have one.

Your kitchen sponge…

Lately, there have been a vocal group of people coming to the defense of the kitchen sponge proclaiming that the sponge is not that bad and that people are giving the sponge a hard time and a bad rap. Well, the sponge deserves that bad rap. It's a breeding ground for bacteria, and an NSF study has confirmed this. The sponge near your sink very likely contains both E. coli and salmonella. Most sponges start harboring both bacteria after three weeks of use, but please, for the love of all things good and noble do not wait three weeks to clean your sponge. You can zap it in the microwave and that will kill most of the E. coli, salmonella, spores and parasites that grow on sponges, but the higher recommendation is to change the sponge out to a new one every two weeks or less. And think about it this way – how much does your sponge actually cost? A dollar or so? How much is your health worth? More than a buck, I'm hoping. Get rid of that nasty sponge and get a new one.

Your bathtub and shower…

Clean your bathtub and shower if you don't want skin lesions or urinary tract infections. Around 26 percent of bathtubs and showers harbor bacteria known as staphylococci. These germs will not just ravish your skin, but will also eat your urinary tract alive if they get their chance. Eliminate their chance of feasting on you by using a mild shower spray on a daily basis.

22 MORE DIRTY LAUNDRY

"I've buried a lot of my laundry in the back yard."
- Phyllis Diller

Laundry is never-ending. And it really doesn't matter if you are the type of person who changes their clothes three times a day or the kind of woman who lives in a uniform wearing the same thing every day. Either way you have to wash what you're wearing. With the exception of jeans – I usually give a pair of jeans three wears before I stick them into the washer. And although I know it sounds a little gross there are actually lots of people who do this – who think that for some reason jeans are a little bit more immune to funk and germs then other clothes. And while it is correct that jeans are more immune to developing funk – they pick up the germs of the world like every other piece of clothing that you wear. However, this doesn't stop people from placing their denim right back into the closet after a long days' wear. Even celebrities have publicly stated that they only wash their jeans once every six months or so. Whatever.

If you live in a household with more than one person and if children are involved then your laundry is endless. And you're probably nanoseconds away from simply throwing all of your clothes in a big bonfire rather than having to do another load.

This is typically how I handle my laundry, which I don't advise for you:

I place one load of laundry in the washer and start it.

I beam proudly that I am doing a

load of laundry, realize how amazing I am, and tell myself that I deserve a treat.

I gorge on chocolate ice-cream bars and peruse the Internet for an hour.

I work a little, eat a little, socialize a little and take off for the rest of the evening.

The next morning I wake up and decide I want to be an amazing laundress and walk into the laundry room to get another load of clothes started.

I realize that the clothes from yesterday are still in the washer.

I assume they are probably slightly stinky and mildewed from sitting in the washer overnight.

I press start on the machine, beam proudly, realize how amazing I am and tell myself that I deserve a treat.

I work a little, eat a little, socialize a

little and take off for the rest of the evening.

The next morning I wake up and decide I want to be an amazing laundress and walk into the laundry room to get another load of clothes washed.

I realize that the clothes from yesterday are still in the washer.

It usually takes me about three days to get one load of laundry done. Enter the husband. Because of his diligence clothes get clean in my house faster. If it weren't for him, no one would have anything to wear.

Here is my advice to you:

Make it a habit to start one load of laundry each day. If you are home all day, I recommend doing laundry in the mornings so that you can get it off your plate early and have your free time to do things that are more important. Also, please remember to separate your clothing from your underwear. Wash your undies alone in extremely hot water. It's more sanitary that way.

We have already covered how beneficial commercial breaks can actually be. And we have discussed that the Fall season should be when your house should be at its cleanest. But the commercial breaks aren't the only thing that is quite helpful in helping a lazy girl get a little bit of housework done. The television is also a prime opportunity to fold laundry.

The great thing about folding laundry is it requires very little cognitive attention. You're picking up socks, putting them together, and folding a shirt over itself. Folding laundry is simplistic enough not to interfere with your television show. So use the commercial breaks for cleaning spurts and television time to fold laundry.

Some lazy girls don't even bother with folding laundry. They just throw their clothing in a drawer – crumpled and wrinkled and could care less if their underwear gets folded. And I have to agree. Folding underwear sounds anal retentive. I actually don't fold mine at all, because it's going on my butt.

The key to keeping laundry under control is to do it as often as possible. If you wait until you have two or more loads to wash then you'll feel exasperated by this chore. I'm sure you've heard a million people tell you that the key to a clean house is to clean as you go. Well this is the same key to keeping laundry under control. Wash clothes as you go.

23 ORGANIZATION

Do you have a place for everything? And I'm not talking about being really crazy and obsessive about where your things are located, as in: phone goes in the left corner of the desk. Laptop remains in the center of desk, penholder is in upper right corner, etc. But just a general idea of where things should go. For example, the penholder, laptop and phone are kept on the desk.

Organization is a useful method in keeping a house clean, cutting back on clutter, and making the cleaning process faster and easier. People also seem to think better in an organized environment. And we are more productive and practical in an organized environment.

If your house is particularly cluttered giving everything a place could be your ticket to become uncluttered. Plastic bins, file folders, cup holders, bookends, CD racks, and anything else that will line all of your stuff up in one neat spot is a good idea. My husband and I had no idea what simply having a bookshelf could do for our lives. Before, our books had been lying around – literally. And then we got a shelf – wham – instant organization and a lot less cleaning – until I get antsy and want to go through my books because I'm bored and feeling like a bookworm.

Get your house organized, and your life just might fall into place. Again, this isn't about being tedious and falling into a frantic meltdown if something is out of place – this is just about having a place for things so that you know where to put the stuff that's lying on the counter and floor.

There are several benefits of having a place for everything. Some of them include:

You always know where to find your stuff. There is nothing more frustrating than needing to leave the house immediately, and you can't find something vitally important like your keys, purse or wallet. This happens to me quite often and is incredibly frustrating. I learned to create a landing strip to keep this from happening. The landing strip is an area in front of my home (near the door) where all of my "I need to leave the house this second or I'll need to go twenty miles above the speed limit" stuff goes. My purse, keys, water bottle, laptop bag are kept on my landing strip, which is in the corner of my kitchen where I can easily pick things up and plop things down as I come and go. Not only should you build your own landing strip, but you should create a strip for everything, so you don't have trouble finding what you need.

Having a place for everything saves time. That deer in the headlights look that occurs when you're holding something in your hands that doesn't have a home is very familiar to me. If you don't have a place for something you'll stand there wondering what you should do with it as the seconds tick away. And if you actually find some place to put it, you'll subconsciously not feel good about it because you still can't be sure if you actually put that thing in the 'right' place. It's up to you to assign everything in your house a place.

There are pros and cons to orderly environment. Apparently, orderly environments somehow propel us to make better and healthier choices in life – but the disorder and chaos also has perks. A disheveled environment is actually scientifically linked to creativity. So take that you neat freaks! I think that some people would be a little surprised that disorder can actually spur a creative mindset. The reason it spurs creativity is because disorderly environments are the antithesis of pure, good social structure, therefore, they compel us to think outside of the box a little more. I try to explain this to my husband every time he asks me to clean my desk.

Which is why it's no coincidence that many creative types, bohemians, free spirits and super busy and productive people have homes that are less than ideal when it comes to organization. But for all the creativity that ensues, this is not necessarily a good thing because a cluttered house is also a reflection of a person's psychological state.

When things have a proper place your home starts to make sense. The feeling that a home is chaotic is actually the feeling that a home doesn't make sense. Part of the chaos can be attributed to things that aren't assigned their place. You'll greatly reduce the chaos in your home by giving things a place, and your home will start to make sense, which means you are on the right path to a peaceful home.

24 FAMILY

One of the best things that a lazy girl has at her disposal are people who love her. Family that urges her to clean her tub after noticing a blackish ring of dead skin and old bath remnants, friends who give her gift certificates for maid services during the holiday season and the most important of all – a husband and children who can help with the cleaning process.

I am a strong believer in assigning chores to children – especially if they are above the age of 11 – which is considered preteen. When children do chores it teaches them valuable life lessons, and it builds lots of character. I was personally doing chores significantly younger. By the age of six, I was scrubbing toilets by hand (my step-father would not allow me the luxury of a brush). Dishes, vacuuming, and cleaning the kitchen from top to bottom were a part of my daily childhood routine, which could be the reason why I don't like to clean now. Yes, I need therapy.

If you have children who can help around the house – folding laundry, putting away dishes, making their OWN beds, then by all means – tell them that they are going to help you out a little bit more. It gets increasingly harder to clean a house as children age. Running behind a toddler and picking up toys is decidedly different than running behind a teenager picking up trash. Of course, not every mother will be able to get their kids on board with the household cleaning – especially if the children are spoiled or stubborn. In this case, you're on your own. Or maybe not, you can always ask your husband.

A husband can be a true asset in

the housecleaning world. My husband is the only reason laundry gets done in my house, and if it were really up to me – my family would likely have to walk around in togas – and by togas I mean wrapped up in bed sheets because actual toga clothing would still be in the laundry basket. If you have a husband who is not incredibly sexist and believes the cleaning is strictly a woman's agenda then there is a chance that he might help you a little. This doesn't necessarily mean that he will help you wash dishes or clean the bathroom floors. But it does mean that there is a possibility that he will put his laundry in the hamper instead of onto the floor or maybe, just maybe, he'll keep his side of the bathroom sink clean. The little things add up.

And if you have a husband that is absolutely phenomenal (and thankfully many husbands actually are) he will go beyond not leaving socks on the floor and actually help you with the dishes every once in a while. And there is something about an attentive, loving husband who is willing to get his hands dirty that makes even the laziest girl want to keep her home clean too – if not for herself – for him. Which leads me to another point.

If you have a family, use them as your motivation. Considering they don't utter the words "I hate you" every day, you can allow them to be your muse, inspiring you to clean and keep your house lovely and spotless. I have to sometimes build myself up and give my morale a boost by telling myself that I'm not cleaning for me – I'm cleaning for people I love, even if I'd be OK with them wearing togas.

25 MOVE IT

For the longest time, we kept our kitchen trashcan in a room that seemed a good mile or two away from our actual kitchen. After a while, I got fed up enough to say that the trashcan needed to move out of the pantry and into the actual kitchen. My kitchen wasn't working for me – I was working for my kitchen.

Rooms work best for us when they are arranged in a way that suits and responds to our needs. Which is why there is nothing worst then a home with a terrible layout. I personally prefer clean, wide-open spaces instead of long corridors and awkwardly placed rooms and sinks.

You can make the cleaning process go faster if you make sure that your home is working for you instead of you working for it. Simple things like ensuring that there is a toilet brush wand next to every toilet can make a world of difference in how easy it is to maintain a clean bathroom. Also, make sure that you keep paper towels and cleaning sprays under every sink of your home, and keep that duster somewhere in the living space (hidden away) so that when it's time to clean the bookshelves you have easy access to it. I even read about a girl who claimed that keeping her vacuum plugged in by the corner of her living room helped her keep the apartment clean. Sure, it's ugly to have a vacuum in your living area and even a bit tacky, but whatever works, right? Determine which objects in your home require the most attention during the cleaning process and then make sure that you place a cleaning tool somewhere near that object.

However, I don't want you to forget about your supply caddy and apron. You should have those things too. But they should be an entirely separate entity. You don't want to go from room to room picking up cleaning tools that are strategically placed around the house. This is simply about having extra stuff for pure convenience. Strategically placed household tools are for easy home maintenance that doesn't require a caddy.

26 KIDS

"Housekeeping is like being caught in a revolving door."
- Marcelene Cox

Living with a child is like living in a frat house. You never know when bodily fluids, food, debris or whatever random item in your house will make it's way somewhere it shouldn't be. I have nieces and nephews who went through phases where they would take important things (like the remote control and hide them). My older brother was missing his remote and some other precious things for weeks before he discovered the toddler had stealthily shoved them in the trunk of tricycle. Who does such a thing? Toddlers and frat boys that's who!

Anybody who tells you that you can

clean your home in five easy steps with a small child is lying to you. And if you believe that you can clean your home in five easy steps with a child then you are lying to yourself. I once read a quote that said cleaning a home with a toddler is like shoveling snow during a snowstorm. That quote couldn't have been more accurate.

With a small child, the rule is quite simple – keep your home clean enough to be healthy, and dirty enough to be happy. And although there are no easy answers for keeping a house clean when you have little ones running around attempting to mess it up quicker than you can clean it… there are things that you can do to make your life a little easier. Below are a few:

Only give your child a few toys to play with. This is about instituting a policy of simplicity. Both you and your baby might think you need a million toys to keep active and busy, but less is more.

Besides, the fewer toys a child has to play with (especially highly intelligent children who are prone to boredom) the less clutter you will have and the more your child will have to use his or her imagination. Too many toys might lead to overstimulation. Fewer toys are good for the brain, and I can only assume that no toys are great for the brain. With this line of thinking, it would make sense to get rid of all the children's toys, but what's great for his brain would be absolutely detrimental to mommy's brain. For moms, toys are the number one culprit that keep a family from enjoying a perfectly clean home. Get rid of toys and store them away, or donate them to another unsuspecting mom. If you're wondering how many toys you should actually have – the answer is enough to fill a toy box.

Contain the toys in one spot. This can be incredibly difficult, especially for children who are very clingy with their parents. They want to play – but they also want to be around you. If this is the case, you'll be spending a lot of time in your child's playroom or bedroom, but you'll have a house that's a tad bit cleaner. Honestly, I don't know if the tradeoff is worth it.

Make children clean up. Even toddlers as young as 15 months can figure out how to pick things up and put them away. Involve your child in the cleaning process as early as possible so that you won't find yourself picking up their stuff until they're 18 – or worse – even older. As your child learns how to pick up their toys and begins to understand the whole cleaning concept – give rewards and punishments for a job well done. A cookie for helping the playroom look nice and tidy – and toy jail for toys that were not picked up after you asked. Children (especially toddlers) take toy jail quite seriously.

27 MUSIC

"I hate housework. You make the beds, you wash the dishes and six months later you have to start all over again."
- Joan Rivers

There are no easy answers for how long you should take to clean your house. This will depend on the speed that you clean and how large your house is. Some people can rush through the cleaning process in a two-bedroom apartment in 15 minutes while other people need an hour. And if you have kids, you can expect to prolong however many hours it would usually take you to clean your home into days. If cleaning your home takes two hours without children, then it will take two days with children. If you have cats or dogs add an extra day.

One great way to make the cleaning process go faster is to play music. I've found that millions of people manage to get through the drudgery of cleaning by playing music. And it also seems that the louder the music is the more bearable the cleaning process is.

What is it about playing music while cleaning that makes it somewhat bearable? There are several reasons, but the most prominent is that music works as an energizer. It doesn't matter if you're playing pop or classical – it's something in the music that can help get you moving, which is why so many people can't imagine hitting the gym without an iPod. If you want to really get into it, consider making your own cleaning soundtrack of songs that you absolutely love.

28 WET ROOMS

I hate cleaning my sink. Especially the kitchen sink, but I also hate cleaning the bathroom sink as well. It's just something about all that wetness that gives me the creeps. Maybe you feel the same way and think that cleaning sinks feels like torture. The worst thing about cleaning bathroom sinks, showers, tubs, and toilets is that they become magnets. When you manage to get them shiny and sparkly your family is sure to want to come and mess it up.

I've noticed a consistent pattern in how cleaning wet rooms attract family, and maybe you've noticed the same pattern in your life. Here is the pattern:

You clean the bathtub or shower. Your husband immediately wants to use that newly cleaned shower or your child wants to play with bubbles and a bath toy (that is actually not a bath toy) in your newly cleaned bathtub. You can't stop them, but you secretly wish that the shower and bathtub could have stayed clean for longer than an hour.

You clean the kitchen sink. Your family decides that now is the time to drop a bowl full of food particles in the sink, and empty out a coffee mug that had been sitting on their desk.

You clean the bathroom sink, and your husband has an incredible urge to shave. Small tiny hairs everywhere – happens every time.

You clean the toilet. Everyone in the house suddenly needs to poop. This also happens every time.

If this is you; I have a suggestion that may or may not work. Before cleaning the toilet, ask everyone in the house if they need to poop; If they say no, don't believe them. Tell them to go in that bathroom and try and push out what they can. Because if they don't poop before you clean, they'll need to poop once you finish cleaning the toilet and when you ask them why they didn't use the toilet before you cleaned it the reply will be a sincere and emphatic "I didn't have to go then."

Ask your husband if he needs to shave before you clean the bathroom sink and make sure that all coffee mugs around the house are in the dishwasher.

And as for the shower and bathtub. Trying to get a man to shower when he doesn't want to is impossible. And trying to get a child to play in the tub when he doesn't want to is equally impossible. You just won't keep your shower or tub clean very long, and you'll need to learn to accept it.

29 STANDARDS

Just because you are lazy doesn't mean that you don't have high standards. Matter of fact, you likely have high standards which is why you're reading this book. You want a clean house, but you just want an easy way to do it. And if you had the money to pay a housekeeper without even blinking at your bank account, then your standards would be immeasurably higher than they already are. High standards are good. It's what keeps you from eating rotten food or marrying a serial killer. People with low standards often find themselves in life-threatening situations.

I don't think that you should lower your standards in any other area except for the area of housecleaning. If you haven't accepted the fact that your house will never be perfect (unless you run into an insane amount of money and can hire a butler to follow you around and wipe up the water that splashes around your sink when you brush your teeth) then you'll just have to accept imperfection.

But you probably also need to learn to let some things slide. This all may sound counterintuitive, considering this is a book that is supposed to whip you in shape. But in addition to whipping you in shape, I also want to give you a reality check and I also want to encourage you not to beat yourself up over the state of your home. There are many things that are far more important.

I did a bit of research by perusing other housekeeping books before writing this one. In many of those books, the author was often preachy and made us lazy girls feel completely inferior for not keeping an immaculate house. Some authors even suggested that we might be driving our husband and children away by not sweeping the floor more thoroughly. Well, I'm here to tell you that you should NEVER sweep a floor. It takes way too much time. Use a vacuum. Or better yet, buy some lazy girl house slippers that have microfiber on the bottom for cleaning the floors as you simply walk around. You may also be able to get dust and debris off your floor with the right pair of socks too.

The good news is that you don't have to be obsessive about keeping your house clean. You can still keep your laid-back persona. There is no need for up-tightness, and I think that life is entirely too short for people to get their panties in a bunch over whether or not the stove is clean. You just have to schedule the right moments for cleaning, moments that work for you and jive with your personality. This will make you AND your home a lot happier and healthier.

30 EXERCISE

Lazy girls don't like to exercise. I absolutely hate it, but lazy girls who gain weight by simply viewing fast food commercials often have to come up with innovative ways to get some exercise in. It works best if we are exercising without actually feeling as if we are exercising. Those of us who despise the treadmill have to set up our schedules to do stuff like go dancing with girlfriends, play tennis, or tag football with our kids. Otherwise, most lazy girls would turn into the kind of lazy girls that have to be airlifted from their homes through the roof if they aren't careful. Fortunately, one great way to get exercise is to house clean. Cleaning can shed quite a few calories. Below are some calorie counts for the average 150lb person. Of course, these counts will vary with weight, intensity and body composition.

If you are a hands and knees girl you can expect to shed as many as 200 calories cleaning your floors. If you don't clean your floors on your hands-and-knees, but you are still working those floors with a mop then expect to expend about 170 calories after 30 minutes of cleaning.

Spend 15 minutes scrubbing your tub and you'll burn 90 calories. Which means that you can eat one very large chocolate chip cookie once you're done.

Vacuuming the home, unfortunately, is seriously labor-intensive, but surprisingly doesn't burn as many calories as most would think. After 30 minutes with a vacuum expect to have burned 119 calories.

Cleaning out the closet for a regular, more organized girl would burn about

85 calories. But if you're super lazy and your closet is a mess, expect to burn twice as much. Just put away those tank tops if winter is coming, and make your shoes look nice and neat.

Cleaning windows are no joke. Expect to burn 167 calories in half an hour.

If you really want a workout, spend some time once a month rearranging your furniture. You'll burn 100 calories every 15 minutes, and it's something about rearranging the furniture that makes a place feel fresh and new. It's almost as if you're pushing any negative energy that's been pent up in certain spots out and giving the space room to breath. I love moving furniture around because of the novelty it brings to my space.

31 THE 1950'S HOUSEWIFE

"Housework is what a woman does that nobody notices unless she hasn't done it."
- Evan Esar

If you ever spent time at your grand-mother or great-grandmother's house when you were little, you probably remember that the way she lived her life was much different from the way that you live yours today. If you are generation X or older, then you probably remember something like this.

You watched her wake up at 5AM and busily clean the kitchen a bit before getting the coffee started in an antique glass percolator. Then you watched as she spent a full hour in the bathroom, putting coats of mascara on her lashes and removing curlers from her hair. By 6:30AM she was starting breakfast, which may have even included freshly baked bread -- from scratch. If your grandfather didn't drink coffee, then your grandmother woke up at 4:30AM because she needed time to squeeze fresh oranges or grapefruit.

If you really want to feel extra bad (or not so bad) about your laziness, I present to you a daily housekeeping schedule of a 1950's wife:

Throw back the covers and go from room to room opening the blinds and windows to allow fresh sunlight into the house

Go to the bathroom to freshen up

Make and serve breakfast

Clean up breakfast

Complete a 10 to 20 minute exercise routine

Bathe, do hair and make-up and get fully dressed (gorgeous and uncomfortable dress and heels)

Find the tidying basket, and go throughout the home picking up items and putting them back in their proper place

Dust, water plants and flowers, straighten and fluff pillows and ensure the living and dining room are perfect

Make the beds and tidy the bedroom, including washing the floors, vacuuming and a light dusting

Clean bathrooms thoroughly, including replacing used towels, refilling toilet paper and soap and cleaning the bathroom countertops or any miscellaneous items that do not belong. Clean the shower, tub and toilet if needed.

Start a load of laundry and set aside any clothes that need special tailoring or a dry cleaner

Review the menu for the current day and make note of anything that needs to be added to the grocery list, and start working on any meals that require lots of preparation – such as meals with marinades

Start long-advance preparations for dinner, including putting together the ingredients necessary for desert

Clean kitchen afterwards includ-ing washing dishes, wiping down kitchen work surfaces, mopping or sweeping kitchen floors and a quick clean of the inside of the fridge

Dispose of garbage

Handle errands such as going to the bank, post office, getting some-thing fixed, correspondence and also add time to volunteer. If there are no errands that need to be completed, and you have completed some volunteer work for the week, indulge in a hobby.

Go to the grocery store, pre-wash all vegetables and fruits and put them away

Have a quick lunch

Handle one weekly chore (which may include polishing silverware, bathroom fixtures, cleaning and disinfecting kitchen appliances or replacing all flowers with fresh bouquets)

Set the table for dinner and the living room for evening enjoyment, such as providing the husband with a newspaper or book

Prepare dinner

Change clothes into something more elegant before the husband arrives home from work

Set out a tray with equipment for making cocktails so that the husband can be served a drink before dinner

Greet husband with a smile and kiss

Serve dinner

Clear table, wash dishes, and pour boiling water down the sink to ensure the pipes are flushed

Pack the husband a nutritious and delicious lunch for the work the next day

Preset the table for tomorrow's breakfast

Start all over again

If you think for a second that things

were significantly easier in the 1960's, think again. In 1962, the hardback cover book that made the bestselling list, and managed to pull in millions was called *Heloise's Housekeeping Hints*. Below are a few of her house cleaning tips:

The best time to clean out your closet is to wait until you're mad. You will say to yourself, "I have kept this dress for two years thinking I would remake it, but I am mad today so why not throw it out?"

Painting the kitchen is best done when your husband is home. If he won't help you at least he can see how hard you worked!

For cleaning house, make a Heloise Sack Blouse from an old bath towel. Fold towel in half, sew up sides, leave opening for arms, make opening for neck. Don't forget the pockets! Grand for housework.

Needs no ironing. Cool in summer, doesn't show water spots, etc. Towels make good shorts, too.

Finally, Heloise makes women feel embarrassingly lazy by giving this tip: "Have you ever noticed how rested you feel after dinner when the dishes are done? This is the time to do some of your hard, time consuming chores."

However, Heloise did have some really great advice such as:

"I wouldn't tell you this is if I though it wasn't worth every little bit of energy you will save... It is not necessary to sweep under your beds every day. Who is going to look under your beds? Save your energy... never waste it."

Leftover potatoes of any type can be mashed and made into delicious "potato patties" for breakfast the next morning. One may also add a chopped onion and an egg. Mix, mash, mold your patties, salt and pepper if you wish, and fry up with a pat of butter. Yum!

Never worry about the necessities. Everybody must pay rent, taxes, and buy necessary foods. Accept the fact that you cannot escape these costs. Save your "worry time" for the things that you buy and don't need!

System is what is needed in housekeeping. If we can't find a system, then the thing to do is get rid of excess things. The less we have, the easier it is to clean.

Don't save your good things for "tomorrow" – use them now. Life is so short – enjoy every day of it.

"Now about washing the tub. Use your broom to do this. Wet the tub and sprinkle cleanser in it. Let the water faucet drip slowly and your old kitchen broom will do the rest for you without you having to stoop over. By using the broom you have accomplished two things with one stroke. You have also washed your broom! "

Remember the paper sack girls, it's used for so many things

32 ALWAYS REMEMBER ...

"At worst, a house unkempt cannot be so distressing as a life unlived"
- Rose Macaulay

A clean house is a constant work in progress. It takes time and effort to have a clean home and it's not as easy as cleaning up one day and hoping that it sticks. A truly clean home requires a life-style change. Fortunately, if you are accustomed to a laid-back kind of life, you can still have a clean home. You just have to do things a bit differently and work with your personality. So get accustomed to using your commercial breaks, don't forget to buy that caddy and some paper plates and cups. And remember, the closet can be your best friend. Just make sure you empty those closet baskets every once in a while, or you may attract spiders.

Don't fret if your house isn't sparkling clean and perfect. Remember that you have more important things to do than clean a house anyway. Besides, no one on their deathbed ever utters the words "I wish I had spent more time cleaning." If anything, people often regret not spending more time with loved ones and doing things that truly mattered and brought joy and peace into their lives. So don't be the uptight person worried about whether or not the TV stand is clean. Instead, make sure that you are investing the bulk of your time in what really matters – and it's not cleaning.